IMAGES OF WALES

RHONDDA

IMAGES OF WALES

RHONDDA

SIMON ECKLEY AND EMRYS JENKINS

TEMPUS

Frontispiece: Blaenrhondda station, 1912. On the hillside in the background, just above the head of the stationmaster, Mr Thomas Brokenbrow, is the old smithy. The blacksmith had a portable forge to visit farms in the area. To indicate when he was in residence and thereby prevent fruitless climbs on the part of potential customers he used to raise a flag on a post outside the building.

First published 1994
Reprinted 1994, 1995
New edition 2003

Tempus Publishing Limited
The Mill, Brimscombe Port,
Stroud, Gloucestershire, GL5 2QG

Captions © Simon Eckley and Emrys Jenkins, 1994
Photographs © Rhondda Borough Libraries and Emrys Jenkins, 1994

The right of Simon Eckley and Emrys Jenkins to be identified as the Authors of this work has been asserted in accordance with the Copyrights, Designs and Patents Act 1988.

British Library Cataloguing in Publication Data.
A catalogue record for this book is available from the British Library.

ISBN 0 7524 3009 2

Typesetting and origination by Tempus Publishing Limited
Printed in Great Britain by Midway Colour Print, Wiltshire

Contents

Workmen building the new Ynysfeio bridge in order to increase the headroom for passing trams, 1926–27. During the recruitment of unemployed men to work on this project preference was given to ex-servicemen, who made up 75 per cent of those taken on.

Introduction

By His Worship the Mayor of Rhondda Borough, Councillor B. Rowland

I was very pleased to be asked to make a contribution to this publication, especially in the Borough's centenary year. Photographs are welcome reminders of our glorious past, and those contained in this publication will, I am sure, provide the reader with much pleasure. Let me take this opportunity to congratulate those responsible for producing this memorable book.

Much has been written and much has been composed about Rhondda and, personally, I always feel inadequate when I am asked to provide a foreword for a publication. On this occasion, however, the photographs say it all and will, I know, evoke nostalgia in the reader.

I am proud to represent Rhondda; I am proud to contribute to this publication which I believe promotes the spirit of Rhondda people. Their struggle and hardship is well known, and from that struggle was born the determination and the will to strive for greater excellence.

Local government in Rhondda was first recorded in 1895 with the inaugural meeting of the Ystradyfodwg District Council taking place in Pentre. One hundred years ago Rhondda was home to a vast mining industry and our prized coal was being exported in huge quantities all over the world taking the fame of these valleys with it. Yet fame was not the only 'attachment' to the industry. Tragedy also followed, and many families were robbed prematurely of their loved ones. Now 'King Coal' lies peacefully beneath us; he no longer reigns, but the fame which he gave Rhondda will continue over the next hundred years and beyond.

In 1996 Local Government reorganisation will force the Borough to merge with our neighbours in Taff Ely and Cynon Valley. I am confident that every endeavour will be made to ensure the continued well-being of Rhondda, to preserve our heritage, and create the necessary conditions for future prosperity and success. Rhondda's dramatic, natural beauty is returning to open a new gateway and to provide new landmarks in our history.

Although the mining era is no longer with us, the unique culture of Rhondda, with its brass bands and choirs and above all our people, will serve both as a living monument to our heritage and as a firm foundation upon which to build and secure a golden future for Rhondda.

There is very little left to say except that in any writing or collection of photographs about Rhondda, the principles of the Borough's motto — 'Fame Outlasts Wealth' — ring true as a record of the spirit of this famous valley. I must now draw to a close but not without first assuring you that as you travel through the following pages you will experience an unforgettable journey which I consider to be a tribute to the history and heritage of Rhondda.

With my best wishes, I remain

B. Rowland.

One
Community

Rhondda Male Choir on the Pittsburg leg of their American tour, 1913. The conductor was Ald. John Phillips J.P. and the accompanist, Mr D.R. James.

Fleet of new Rhondda Transport double-decker buses at the Porth depot, 1934, shortly before they entered into service. The increase in the popularity of the buses led to the abandonment of the tramway system in the Rhondda Fawr (31 December 1933) and the Rhondda Fach (1 February 1934). Yet the changeover did not pass without an outburst of nostalgia for as the last tram rolled into the depot a large crowd broke into *Farewell my own true love*.

Above: Rhondda Valley Terrier Association, 1932. Front row (third from right) is Will Evans ("Dogs") and in the third row, standing behind the cups, his brother, Trevor Evans.

Right: The "Six Welsh Miners", a group of former miners from the Rhondda Fach who toured the country as singers during the 1920s.

Officers of the 7th Glamorgan Battalion of the Home Guard, Drill Hall, July 1944. The picture was taken at a ceremony marking the 65th birthday of the Glamorgan Home Guard's commanding officer, Lt.-Col. John Evans J.P., who was presented with a silver cigarette box and pipe.

Opposite above: Mayor of the newly created Borough of Rhondda, Mr J.G. Elias J.P., Deputy Mayor Mrs Elizabeth Jones and the long serving Clerk of the Council, Mr D.J. Jones (1928-58) follow the mace bearer during the first Mayor's civic service, Bethesda Congregational chapel, Ton Pentre, 24 July 1955.

Opposite below: Civic Sunday parade in Ferndale for the 1958-9 Rhondda Borough Mayor, Cllr. Evan Edwards.

Ald.Ivor Idris Jones, last chairman of Rhondda Urban District Council 1954–55, sits in the chain of office surrounded by his councillors.

Mr Thomas R. Davies of Tonypandy holding the freedom casket presented to him at his home in December 1955. Mr Davies (Chair of Rhondda UDC, 1929-30) and Mr Mark Harcombe, B.E.M. of Trealaw (Chair of Rhondda UDC, 1922-23), both distinguished former civic leaders, were in 1955 made the first Freemen of the new Borough of Rhondda.

two

Blaenrhondda
to Treherbert

Workmen on the Blaencwm railway tunnel, late 1880s. By 1880 steam coal exports from the Rhondda collieries were becoming increasingly restricted through the monopoly enjoyed by the Taff Vale Railway and the Bute Docks at Cardiff. This led rival mine owners to press for additional rail links to the sea and by 1914 new railways had been built connecting the Rhondda with Barry, Port Talbot, Swansea and Newport. The directors of the Rhondda and Swansea Bay Company, incorporated in 1882, were determined to link the upper Rhondda Fawr to the ports of Swansea Bay. Work on the Blaencwm tunnel, which connected Treherbert and Cymmer in the Afan Valley, began in June 1885 and was completed on 2 July 1890. At 3,300 yards it was then the seventh longest tunnel in Britain. However, the new line failed to live up to the expectations of its promoters; with prices for steam coal generally higher at Cardiff, Barry and Newport and the disadvantage of the gradient (heavy coal trucks having to negotiate the slope up the valley) the Rhondda and Swansea Bay Company ended by serving only those collieries at the very top of the Rhondda Fawr.

View of Penyrenglyn and Treherbert, *c.*1900, with Ynysfeio Colliery and its massive tip dominating the old farmhouse. Sinkers' huts are on the right while the houses on Baglan Street and Ynyswen Road have as yet been built on only one side.

Blaenrhondda entrance to the Llyn Fawr tunnel, c.1909, showing a gang of miners employed by Messrs W.M. Treglown & Co., the contractors for the project. The Llyn Fawr reservoir, completed in 1910 with a capacity of 202 million gallons, was a key element in the efforts of Rhondda Urban District Council to improve the appalling sanitary conditions in the Rhondda and "provide a proper and sufficient supply of water to the district". During the Second World War the tunnel, a potential target for enemy sabotage, had to be permanently guarded and two members of the Home Guard, brothers Will and Herbie Jenkins were detailed for a spell of duty there. With only one rifle between them and no ammunition they took turns, one holding the rifle for a while and the other the bayonet. By tapping messages on a water pipe they could keep in touch and warn of impending danger. If anyone was foolish enough to approach the tunnel the brothers would have to run back towards each other and quickly replace the bayonet on the rifle so that they could issue the challenge of "who goes there?"

Opposite above: Train passing along the Rhondda and Swansea Bay Railway line in the direction of the Blaencwm tunnel, c.1900. It used to be a regular practice for the mothers of children suffering from whooping cough to shove the child's head out of the carriage window as the train passed through the tunnel. The fumes were supposed to provide an effective cure!

Opposite below: Dr Hinde with his driver William Watts, Blaencwm, c.1910. In A.J. Cronin's *The Citadel*, which drew heavily on his experiences as a doctor in the Rhondda and elsewhere in South Wales, the character of Dr Page was largely based on Hinde. Cronin was Hinde's assistant around 1920 and briefly lodged with him and his wife at Tynewydd cottage.

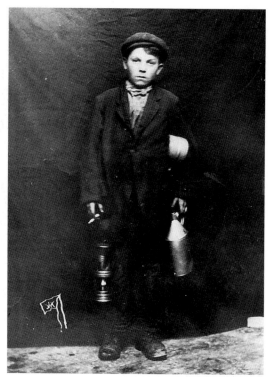

Left: Henry Cambell who worked as an ostler at the Ynysfeio Colliery, *c.*1910. His left hand rests on a numbered log indicating that it was "block day", always a Tuesday and Thursday, on which colliers were allowed to cut and bring home two blocks each for use as firewood. *Right*: Jim Cambell, son of Henry, pictured before the start of his first day's work at Ynysfeio Colliery, *c.*1910.

Penyrenglyn Infants School, 1953-4.

Crowds awaiting the arrival of King George V and Queen Mary during the first visit by a reigning monarch to the Rhondda, Treherbert station, 27 June 1912. The railings ensured the separation of the hoi polloi from the dignitaries on the platform itself.

Gwilym Williams, newsagent's, 25 Baglan Street, Penyrenglyn, c.1915. Mrs Alice Williams and her three children are pictured.

Co-op Square, Treherbert, *c.*1920, with the Treherbert branch of the Ton co-operative (right) and Isaac Jones' printers' shop (established 1872) on the left. Jones, developed a business as one of the leading printers in Wales during the last quarter of the nineteenth century. He was the only music publisher in the Rhondda and printed most of the *Cymanfa Ganu* pamphlets and choir music for the valleys. His old printing presses are now on display at the Rhondda Heritage Park.

Children's soup kitchen established alongside the National School, Penyrenglyn during the miners' lockout of 1921. Mr Dillwyn Jones (extreme left) was responsible for finances, ordering of food, and any other requirements. Adults, meanwhile, had their own separate kitchen at the Carmel chapel, Baglan Street.

Jimmy Jones, chauffeur for the model T. Ford of Mr T.L. Mort, colliery agent, outside the Opera House, Treherbert, 1920s.

No.1 and No. 2 pits, Fernhill Colliery, Blaenrhondda with, to the right, Office Row (demolished July 1962) and, in the background, Fernhill Houses (demolished 1963-4). Living in the middle of a colliery made wash-day particularly hazardous. Housewives would carefully watch which way the wind was blowing before hanging out the washing and when the clothes had dried they would be vigorously shaken to remove the coal dust. A typical Fernhill joke has a overman urging on a collier late for work, "Come on Dai the hooter's gone!". The reply: "who the hell pinched that then?".

View of Treherbert, 1920s, with the now demolished St Mary's church clearly visible top left. This was erected by the Marquis of Bute in 1868 at a cost of £4,000. Other buildings of interest which have since disappeared are the foundry (bottom left), Emmanuel chapel (centre) and to the right, the Opera House and the Railway Hotel.

Station Street, Treherbert, c.1925. The Opera House on the right operated from 1872 until 1934 when it was gutted by fire. St Mary's church is in the background.

Iris Evans, Treherbert Hospital carnival queen accompanied by her maids of honour, 1933.

"Simon Peter" passion play held at St Mary's, Easter 1940. From left to right, back row: Mansel Davies, Mr Howells, Revd Jeffson Phillips, Mr Pearce, -?-, Mr Pratt, Revd Horace Davies, J.M. Jones, Walter Murray (organist). Second row: Frank Haddock, Polly Morgan, Maggie Lines, Joan Thomas, Revd I.Roberts, Mrs Roberts, Jack Addis, Jessie Biggs, Mary Miles, Bayne Biggs. Front row: Lawrence Howells, Ada Doughty, Glenys Anderson, -?-.

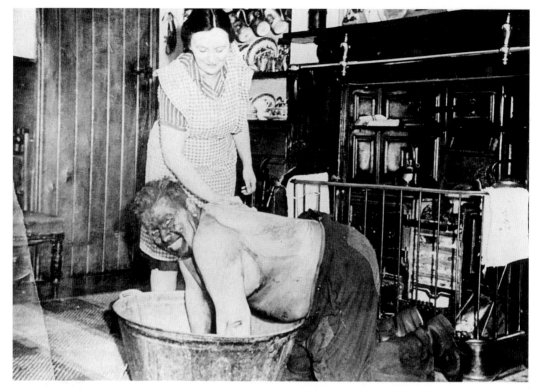

Emlyn Jones of Tynewydd having his back scrubbed by his wife, Agnes after finishing his shift at the pit, *c*.1948. The picture originally appeared in one of the national dailies along with an article on coping with the post-war soap shortage. As a result of the coverage the Joneses were inundated with parcels of soap, some from as far afield as the Yukon and the United States!

General View Treherbert Swimming Pool.

Swimming baths at Treherbert, *c*.1950, with Penpych looming in the distance and the Bute Colliery just visible top left.

Pegler's Stores, Treherbert, 1952.

Black and White Toppers jazz band outside the Railway Hotel, Station Street, Treherbert, *c*.1954. The band leader was Emma Bryant.

The Duke of Edinburgh listens to spontaneous singing of Calon Lân by surface workers at Fernhill Colliery, 28 April 1955. The Duke was visiting the Rhondda to present the Charter of Incorporation elevating the Rhondda to the status of a Municipal Borough. In his address Prince Phillip remarked that "it is hard to compute the contribution which this mining community has made to the power and prosperity of the United Kingdom" and the aquisition of Borough status was widely welcomed as just reward for decades of determined labour on the part of the men and women of the two valleys.

Treherbert Town women's football team at the celebrations organized to mark Prince Charles' Investiture as Prince of Wales, July 1969.

three

Treorchy and
Cwmparc

View of Treorchy, *c.*1900, with Tyl-y-coch and part of Abergorky Colliery on the near side of the railway line. Gilnockie House, now the site of Treorchy library and the Parc and Dare Hall, is clearly visible on the right bank of the river.

Treorchy quoits team, *c*.1910.

Short's shop also known as The Bee-Hive,
128 High Street, Treorchy, *c*.1920. Pictured
together with an unknown assistant (right) are
Mr David Lewis Short, his wife, Catherine and
their two children, William and Katie. During
the bombing of Cwmparc (see p.38) the windows
were blown out, and remained boarded up until
the demolition of the shop in 1986. A doctor's
surgery has now been built on the site.

First session of Treorchy Parliamentary Debating Society, 1924. Many of the members went on to join the Independent Labour Party. Meetings were held above the wine stores in Regent Street, Treorchy.

Fourth from the left in the front row is Hughie Davies of Treherbert, renowned for his monologues.

Rt. Hon. Will John (third from the left), MP for Rhondda West (1920-50), seen here standing next to Dr John Armstrong at Pentwyn Cottage Hospital, shortly after its opening in January 1925. John, one-time chairman of the Cambrian Strike Committee, had been imprisoned for his involvement in the crisis of 1910-11 (see p.72). The hospital was originally maintained by a penny in the pound deduction from the wages of Ocean employees.

Cwmparc Silver Band (now the Parc and Dare Band), 1926.

Opening ceremony of the National Eisteddfod held at Treorchi in 1928. Raising the Welsh flag is David Davies (later Lord Davies of Llandinam), mine-owning philanthropist and grandson of one of the great Welsh pioneers of the Rhondda coalfield, David Davies, Llandinam, founder of the Ocean Coal Company in 1887.

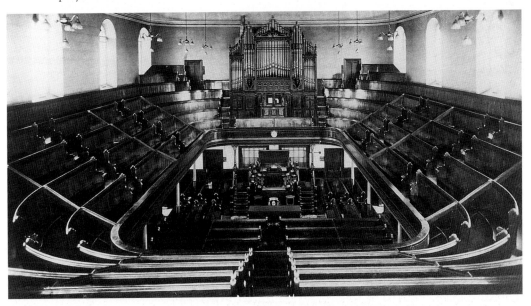

Interior of the now demolished Noddfa Baptist chapel, High Street, Treorchy, 1929. In the period 1860 to 1914 the religious, cultural and, in many ways, the political life of the Rhondda was generated and dominated by the Welsh nonconformist chapel. In 1914 there were 151 chapels within the Rhondda Urban District with seating for 85,000! Between the wars, however, the chapels increasingly saw their position as centres for community life usurped by the Miners' Institutes and Working Men's Clubs.

David Lloyd George, his wife and daughter Megan together with nine-year-old Miss Evie Williams, winner of the folk song competition at the National Eisteddfod, Treorchi, 1928.

Treorchy RFC, 1935.

End of Parc Colliery "stay down" strike, October 1935. The men had remained underground for eight days in protest at the employment of "scab" union men. Iorrie Thomas MP is standing on the far right and Will May, the miners' agent is on the left in the leather coat. Behind the men are members of the lodge committee among them Fred Emery, Humphrey Prosser, Ben Butler (in white coat) and Ned Lampey.

Treharne Street, Cwmparc after the German bombing on the night of 29–30 April 1941. Six people were killed by a direct hit on No. 51, including Nurse Elizabeth Ann Jones of Treorchy, a special constable, three evacuees and a mother. In total the death toll inflicted that night on the village of Cwmparc amounted to twenty-eight.

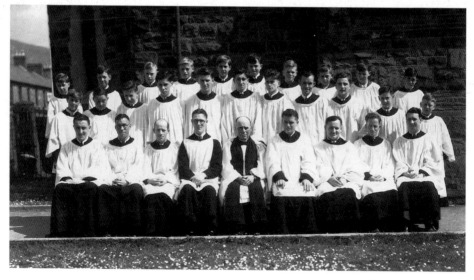

St Matthew's church choir, *c.*1950, with Revd E.J.Howells (centre of front row). Originally a national school, the building was enlarged and converted into a church in 1884. Services were conducted in English and Welsh until 1895 when St Tyfodwg's church was built to cater for the needs of the Welsh speaking population.

Canteen at Polikoff clothing factory, Treorchy, *c*.1950. The prolonged period of economic depression and mass unemployment in the late 1920s and 1930s had clearly shown up the weaknesses of Rhondda's lop-sided industrial structure centred almost exclusively on coal. In 1921 the census returns revealed that 66.7 per cent of males over twelve years of age were employed in coal mining but as demand for coal fell, so too did the number of miners employed in Rhondda's inefficient collieries; from 39,777 in 1927 to 19,873 in 1936. Diversification was called for in order to "absorb" the unemployed and to stem the flood of economic refugees fleeing the valleys. Under the Special Areas Act of 1934 an attempt was made to open new factories in the South Wales coalfield. However, although the new Treforest Industrial Estate (established 1936) did provide jobs for some in the lower Rhondda it was not until 1939 that the first factory buidings were completed and occupied within the Rhondda itself. Through the efforts of town clerk, David J. Jones ("D.J.") Messrs Alfred Polikoff (Wales) Ltd began large scale clothing manufacture at Ynyswen, Treorchy while at Dinas, Flex Fasteners Ltd opened for the production of zips. Nevertheless, such efforts, welcome though they were, had merely scratched the surface and it took the demands of war to wipe away Rhondda's dire unemployment problem.

Polikoff factory, *c.*1950. The building covered
80,000 square feet and was designed to
accomodate 1,500 workers.

Boots chemist, 123 Bute Street, Treorchy,
1953. The Treorchy branch of the Ton
Co-operative stood next door.

Treorchy RAFA Songsters, 1962. From left to right, back row: T. Owen, J. Watkins, J. Hodder, P. Knapgate, R. Evans, B. Reynolds, E. Taylor, A. Pickens, N. Rees. Second row: R. Morris, N. Taylor, M. Jones, D. Morgan, L. Evans, T. Hughes, G. Davies, R. Maddocks. Front row: E. Williams, R. Harry, I. Morgan (pianist), E.T. Jones (conductor), D. Jones, E. Jenkins, C. Jones. Formed in 1960 to raise money for the Royal Air Force Benevolent Fund, the success of the evening turned a one-off venture into a permanent group holding regular weekly rehearsals. The Songsters gave concerts at Rhondda hospitals and old people's homes, the high point of their career together coming with the invitation in 1962 to open proceedings at the RAFA annual conference in Llandudno with the singing of the national anthems.

Joe Loss jokes with the girls and signs autographs in the machine shop during his visit to the EMI factory, Treorchy, 1976. An EMI recording star and well-known bandleader, Joe's signature tune was *In the Mood* and there is little doubt that he was, as he boogies here with Lil Eliott.

First wedding to be held at the Catholic church, Treorchy, 1919. From left to right, back row: Freddie Thomas, Lizzie Murphy, Andrew O'Sullivan (also seen at work on page 16). Front row: Mary Murphy, Ernest Crabb (groom), Gwladys Walters (bride), Alice Thomas.

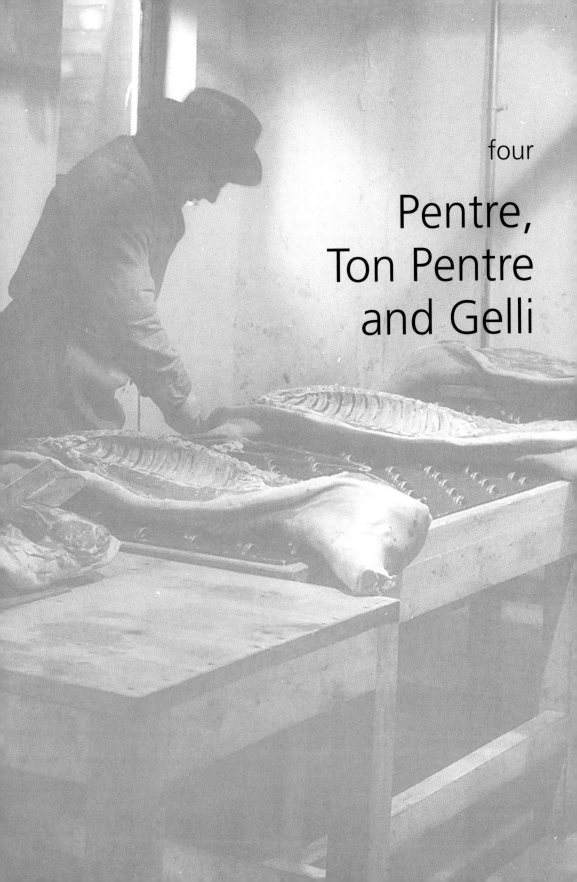

four

Pentre, Ton Pentre and Gelli

General view of Pentre, *c*.1900, with St Peter's church, the "cathedral" of the Rhondda, centre left. This was built between 1888 and 1890 at a cost of £20,000 by Griffith Llewellyn of Baglan Hall. In the

foreground are the mining engineering works of Llewellyn and Cubitt, now "the Barracks", and to the centre right the spoil heap of Pentre Colliery.

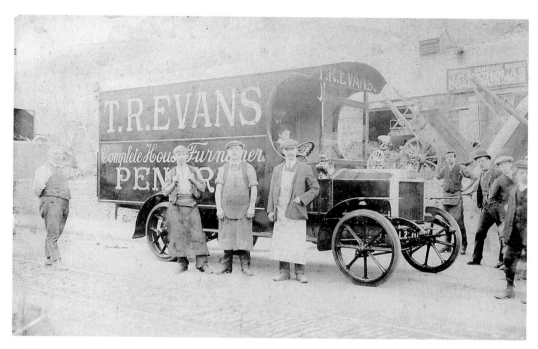

Staff and delivery van of T.R. Evans, House Furnishers, *c*.1900.

Mr Mack the manager, outside the King's Hall
(commonly known as "The Bug and Flea Pit"),
Ystrad Road, Pentre, *c*.1910.

Cory Workmen's band, Pentre, winners of the South Wales Shield Championship and National Eisteddfod, 1911

Pentre Colliery, first opened in 1864, seen here *c.*1915. In 1869 the colliery was bought by the powerful Cardiff ship owners John and Richard Cory who soon extended their mining interests in the Rhondda with the purchase of the Gelli and Tynybedw pits. Their intention was to establish a global network of coal depots and agencies and with Welsh steam coal fuelling the steamships of the world they owned 80 bunkers by the time of John Cory's death in 1910. On the eve of the First World War South Wales was the source of roughly a third of the world's coal trade, the Rhondda alone producing 9.6 million tons a year.

Church Road, Ton Pentre, *c*.1905. The Windsor Castle public house can be seen in the distance with its columned porch.

Llewellyn Street, Pentre, *c*.1920.

Gelli Park shortly after its opening in 1919 by Councillor Jim James of Ystrad. From left to right: Jack Smith, Ray Williams, Tom Thickens, Dai Sargent, Frank Baber, Billy Pritchard, Mr Gammon the park-keeper, -?-, Benny Jenkins, later manager of the Grand Theatre, Pentre and the Empire Theatre, Tonypandy,-?-. For many years after Mr Gammon's "reign" all the park-keepers were referred to as "the Gammon".

Gelli AFC, 1920-21 season.

Right: The Duke of York, later George VI, seen here driving from the first tee of Ton Pentre golf course, 17 May 1924. President of the club at the time was Major Fergus Armstrong, the well-known Rhondda doctor.

Below: Bridgend Square, Ton Pentre, after the erection of the Belisha beacons. Note the woman carrying her baby in a shawl in the Welsh fashion.

Opening of Tyishaf Road railway bridge, Gelli, 1933.

Pentre Secondary Grammar School rugby team, 1939-40 season.

Pentre Secondary Grammar School hockey team, 1946-7 season.

Chairing the bard at Pentre Secondary Grammar School, 1947. The Urdd National Eisteddfod was held in Treorchi that year.

Messrs Cule & Son Ltd provide Father Christmas with a "sleigh" for the 1949 parade.

Pupils at Bronllwyn School Gelli, 1951, re-enacting the miners' meetings of the pre-war years when thousands gathered to hear the fiery oratory of union leaders such as A.J. Cook.

Festival of Britain celebrations in Clara Street, Gelli, 1951.

A packed house attending one of the concerts organised for the Rhondda Music Week held between 4 and 9 June 1951 as part of the Festival of Britain. The marquee was erected on the old Pentre Colliery site.

Pentre House and Cottage, viewed from the top of St Peter's church, *c.*1950. The house was demolished in the late '60s and is now the site of an old people's home.

Hutchings' Bacon Factory, 1954.

Above: Pentre library, 1960s. Formerly a technical school the building served as the central library and administrative offices of the Rhondda Library Service from 1940 until 1971, when new purpose-built headquarters were opened in Treorchy.

Right: Humpback bridge over the Maindy Colliery railway line, Ton Pentre, *c*.1970, pictured shortly before its demolition to allow road improvements. Naish dentist's surgery is shown on the brow of the hill.

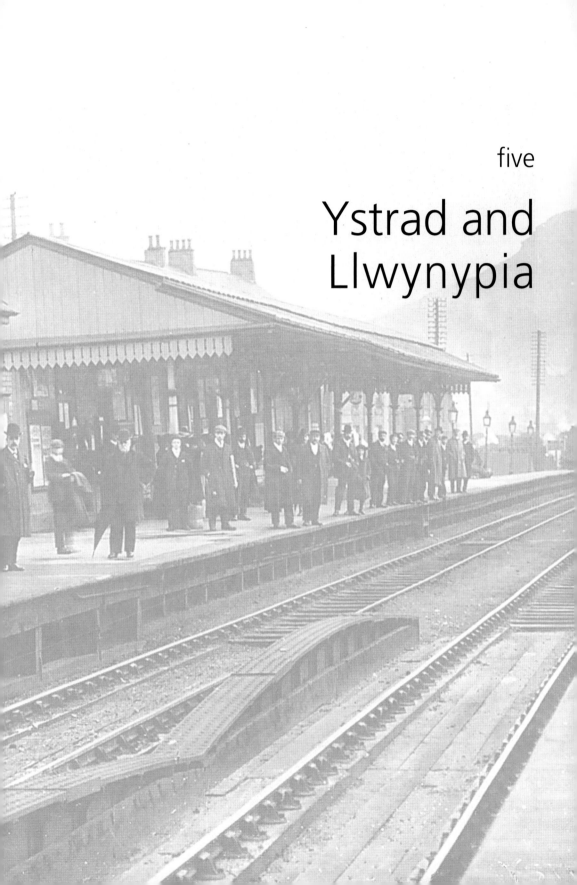

five

Ystrad and Llwynypia

William Street, Ystrad, *c*.1895, with Mrs Shortman unpacking china outside her shop. Mr Shortman's barber shop was next door and the Bodringallt Arms opposite.

Glamorgan Collieries, Llwynypia, *c*.1900 with the Miners' Library and Institute to the right. The pits here were later integrated into the Cambrian Combine of D.A. Thomas MP (Viscount Rhondda) and were the scene of violent clashes during the "Tonypandy Riots" of 1910 (see p.72).

Sculptor Walter Merritt pictured close to the completion of his statue of Archibald Hood (1823–1902). The finished work was erected in front of Llwynypia Miners' Library and Institute in 1906 and unveiled by William Abraham MP (Mabon), Rhondda's first MP from 1885 until 1920. Hood was a Scottish mining engineer and colliery proprietor of some repute who came to South Wales in 1860. Here he played a major part in the development of the Rhondda coalfield notably at the Glamorgan Coal Company's pits at Llwynypia where the colliery was actually known as "the Scotch" in his honour.

Ystrad Juniors AFC, 1913-14 season.

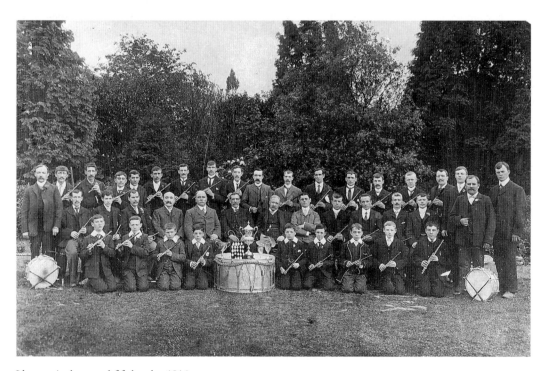

Llwynypia drum and fife band, c.1914.

Master and members of Ystrad Hunt, 1915-16. Hunting remained a popular activity in the Rhondda uplands into the industrialised era with packs at Tynewydd, Ystrad and Tyn-y-cymmer in addition to the famous Glôg (or Llanwynno) Hounds. In the pastoral society, before exploitation of the coalfield, hunting was seen by the Rhondda hillmen and farmers as both a necessary pest control and a major sport. Such was the reputation of these *Gwŷr y Gloran* (men of the "tail") that the name was applied generally to all the inhabitants of pre-industrial Rhondda.

Pontrhondda Girls School, 1915.

Ystrad station, 1921. The Taff Vale Railway had been opened for passenger service as far as Ystrad in 1861 and two years later it was extended to Treherbert.

Matron and staff of Llwynypia Hospital on a charabanc trip, 1932.

Above: Ystrad library before the war. Opened in 1895, it stood on the river bank opposite the Gelli collieries of Cory Bros Ltd for whose men it catered. On the night of 29/30 April 1941, however, it was destroyed during the German air raid on Cwmparc and Ystrad. The explosion completely demolished the building, killing Mrs Roach the caretaker, and severely damaged the surrounding houses on Ystrad Road.

Left: Removal work at the Ynyscynon tip, 1947. By September 1948 the area had been completely cleared.

Apprentice Emrys Jenkins setting and operating the capstan lathe at Pontrhondda Technical College, Llwynypia, 1948.

Opposite above: Ystrad Rhondda and Bodringallt schools, 1940s.

Opposite below: Tyntyla Hospital staff, 1952. It served as the isolation hospital for the Rhondda with beds for 100 patients.

Staff of Royal London Mutual Insurance Society, Ystrad, 1952. Back row: W. Harterre, F. Criddle, S.V. Roberts, H. Morris, W.K. Elliott, N. Parry, R. Chamberlain. Front row: C.H. Owen, R. Miles, T.R. Broad, S.J. Higgon (Superintendant), L.M. Elliott (Clerk-Cashier), A. Thomas, T.R. Jones.

Bamford Spring Interiors Ltd, Llwynypia, 1953. This factory was part of the efforts of the post war Labour goverment to coax new light industries into the Rhondda and other "development areas" in an attempt to widen and strengthen the economic base in the valleys (see p.40).

The Star Hotel, Ystrad, 1960s. Situated at the foot of the Penrhys road connecting the Fawr and the Fach this is the oldest established hostelry in the Rhondda Valleys. An old "joke" about the hotel goes as follows, A: What's the highest mountain in the world? B: It must be Mount Everest. A: No, no, Penrhys of course, because it's above the Star!

Mel Hopkins, who at sixteen joined Tottenham Hotspur direct from Ystrad Boys' Club. He was a regular member of the Spurs side from 1952 to 1964 and as a rangy full-back was capped 34 times for Wales, playing an important role in the legendary Welsh team which reached the quarter-finals of the 1958 World Cup in Sweden. In 1994 Mel was accepted into the Welsh Sporting Hall of Fame.

The Terraces, Llwynypia, c.1964. Intended to house the workers of Archibald Hood as close as possible to the colliery site they were built to the highest standards of the time (1860s) incorporating wide windows and private gardens.

Harold Wilson, then Leader of the Opposition, during a 1971 visit to the Penrhys estate. This complex had been built in the 1960s to improve the quality of housing available in the Rhondda. Wilson was later that day a guest speaker at a civic dinner for Cllr. B.J.Jones (Gelli).

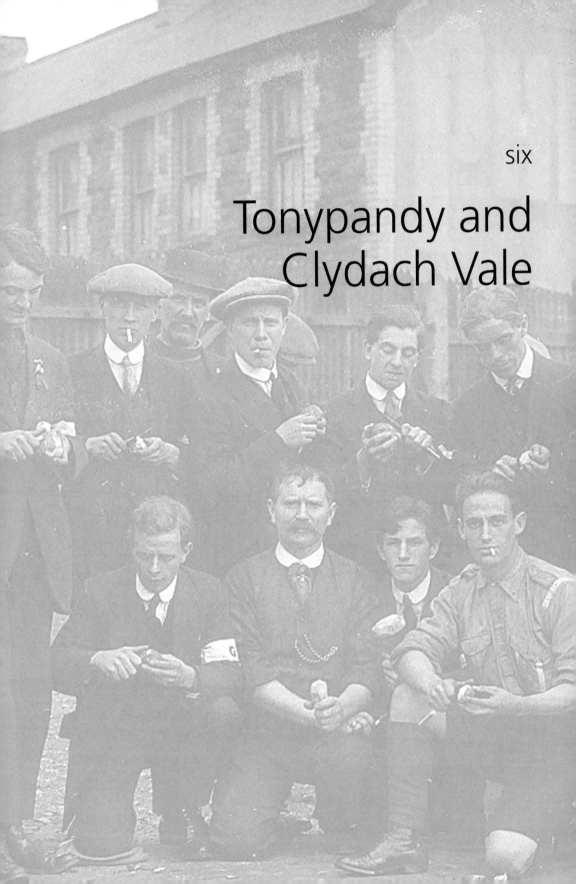

six

Tonypandy and Clydach Vale

Adam Street after severe flooding, Clydach Vale, 10 March 1910. One woman and five children were killed when water, which had been dammed up in a disused coal level, rushed down the hillside demolishing the pictured house and flooding a nearby schoolyard. The boundary wall of the playground collapsed and many of the children were caught up in the water, a far greater disaster only being averted by the quick thinking and bravery of teachers, and passing colliers on their way home from the pits.

View of a church "walk", Thomas Street, Blaenclydach, c.1910.

Clydach Vale Democratic Club Distress Committee, 1910, helping to reduce the suffering of the families of miners involved in the Cambrian Strike.

Zion Hill, Tonypandy with "the Huts" centre left, *c.*1910. Pandy Terrace and Cwrt Square ("the Huts") were wooden houses with slate roofs built around 1890. They were demolished in the 1960s and the site is now occupied by Mitchell Court.

CARDIGANSHIRE POLICE   TONYPANDY COALSTRIKE 1911.

Cardiganshire police despatched to the Rhondda to maintain order during the infamous Cambrian strike, 1910–11. The dispute had begun over piece rates for a new and stony coal seam at the Ely pit, Penygraig controlled by the Cambrian Combine. Following the lock-out of all 950 workers at the pit, the union, the South Wales Miners' Federation, in a great show of solidarity called out on strike all 12,000 men employed by the Cambrian Combine. With the mine owners desperate to avoid flooding in the now deserted pits blackleg labour was imported to operate the pumps and ventilation systems. This provoked bitter anger on the part of the striking miners and on 7 and 8 November 1910 tension bubbled to a head leading to skirmishes with police at the Glamorgan Colliery, Llwynypia and more serious clashes in Pandy Square, which resulted in the death of one striker from a fractured skull and injuries on both sides — the "Tonypandy riots". Under the orders of Home Secretary Churchill the area was swamped with troops and "ringleaders" arrested. Meanwhile the strike dragged on until the widespread suffering of the men and their families forced a return to work in September 1911, on terms offered the previous October.

The Square, Tonypandy, *c.*1912. On the left was the chemist's of William John Richards The hairdresser's to the right was knocked down in the 1920s to allow the widening of the road to Clydach Vale.

Spud drill by the Glamorgan National Reserve, Tonypandy, 1914. The reserve was assembled to provide some rudimentary military training for those who might be required for active service. The commanding officer of the Rhondda battalion was Col. Leonard Llewelyn.

Butchers' auction, Clydach Vale, 1915 in aid of the Red Cross. Mr Hutchings, founder of Hutchings, Ton Pentre (see p.55) can be seen seventh from the left in the black derby.

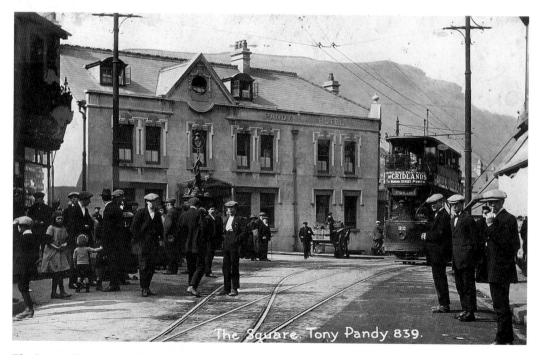

The Square, Tonypandy with a rebuilt Pandy Hotel, 1920s.

Tramcar in Dunraven Street, Tonypandy, *c*.1910.

The Pandy Square Fountain, commonly known as "the Lady with the Lamp" or more colourfully as the "Last Virgin in Pandy" seen here in the workshop of its constructors, Messrs Coalbrookdale Co. Ltd, Coalbrookdale, Shropshire, 1909. It was financed with the money left over after the erection of the statue of Archibald Hood (see p.59).

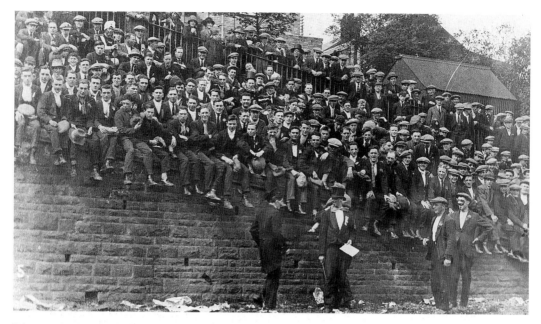

"Catty and Doggy" tournament at the Oval, Tonypandy, 1926. The game, based on an old children's pastime, was played in an open space around the "dab" or makeshift wicket, normally a pile of stones, using customised mandrel sticks. The shorter "catty", sharpened at both ends, was approximately 5-6 inches long with the "doggy" or bat between 18 and 20 inches. Competitions were held to raise funds for miners' families and to provide entertainment during the long 1926 strike.

Charabanc outside the "Bracchi" shop, 5 De Winton Street, Tonypandy, *c.*1923. Established by Julio Bracchi in the 1890s this was the first Italian shop to trade in the Rhondda and thereafter, the name Bracchi was applied to all the Italian shops in the Valleys whatever the name of the proprietor. With the death of Mr Bracchi the shop was taken over by Ernesco Melardi.

J.D. Jones & Sons' fruit, vegetable and fish shop, Dunraven Street, Tonypandy, *c.*1936. J.D. Jones is pictured in the apron with his assistant, Phil Coleman.

Tommy Farr in training camp seclusion, Long Branch, New Jersey, 1937. He is seen here being presented with a Welsh flag by the Mayor of Long Branch, Alton Evans, himself a Welshman. He granted Farr the Freedom of the City and arranged a band to provide a magnificent American reception for the challenger. Farr fought five contests in New York in the late 1930s beginning on 30 August 1937 with the legendary duel for the Heavyweight Championship of the World with "Brown Bomber", Joe Louis. This fight, though lost on points after fifteen rounds, established Farr's reputation as the greatest heavyweight ever to be produced by this country.

S. Hopkins, fruit merchant, Clydach Vale, *c.*1950.

"The Lights", Dunraven Street, Tonypandy, with the Central Hall on the right, 1960s.

seven

Penygraig
and Trealaw

A good example of a Welsh longhouse at Dinas Isaf Farm, Penygraig.

Penygraig Co-operative van, *c.*1910 with Mr Richard Henshaw, his son David and daughter Nan. The first co-op stores in the Rhondda was established in 1868 at Treorchy.

The Square, Partridge Road, Trealaw, *c.*1910.

All Saints' garden party, Trealaw, 1912.

Golden Age bridge, Williamstown, *c.*1905.

THE KING & QUEEN LEAVING THE RESCUE STATION DINAS. 27-6-1

Visit by George V and Queen Mary to Dinas rescue station during their whistle stop tour of South Wales, 27 June 1912.

Laying of foundation stone for St Barnabus' church by Mrs Hughes, wife of the Bishop of Llandaff, 19 February 1914. The church was built at a cost of £2,500 and seats 325 people.

Loading tarmacadam at the Council's destructor works, Dinas, 1930s.

Clinker being taken out for burning at the destructor works, Dinas, 1930s. Clinker was the residue left after burning household rubbish. Crushed, and mixed with tar and bitumen, it could then be used for road surfacing.

Penygraig Naval Colliery, 1940s, now the site of Penygraig RFC's ground.

Welfare Foods' publicity at Trealaw Nursery School, 1949 with members of the Trealaw Food Control Committee seated in the front row. Young Rhondda children at this time received daily doses of cod liver oil and orange juice, either at school or from the various clinics in the area.

An attentive congregation listens to Mrs Markham at the House o' the Trees, Williamstown, c.1950. In an attempt to alleviate some of the hardship caused by the Depression the Salvation Army's League of Goodwill had established the House o' the Trees at Penrhiwfer in 1932. Under the leadership of Major and Mrs Markham hundreds of unemployed youths received training in various trades. During the war years the settlement housed large numbers of evacuees and from 1942 it was used as a training centre for young delinquents.

Group of boys with Salvation Army officer at the House o' the Trees, *c.*1950.

Trealaw Nursery School, *c.*1950.

Pupils at Craig-yr-Eos School, Penygraig busy working on their Coronation year history project, 1953.

Tylacelyn Road, Penygraig, *c.*1955.

Appletree, Dinas, *c.*1960, showing the new blocks of flats which replaced some of the nineteenth century housing in the area.

Concrete houses, Dinas, 1960.

eight

Porth

Porth Junior School, 1905.

Lewis Merthyr Collieries, Trehafod, *c*.1910. This area was first developed in the 1850s with the Hafod and Coedcae collieries working the upper bituminous seams. Between 1880 and 1881 three great steam coal pits were sunk, the Bertie, Trefor and Hafod Pits. By 1900 all these collieries had been united under the control of William Thomas Lewis (1837-1914), Lord Merthyr from 1911. Production boomed to nearly a million tons annually and the Lewis Merthyr Collieries Company Ltd. became one of the most important mining concerns in Britain. Eight years after its closure in 1983 Lewis Merthyr was re-opened as the Rhondda Heritage Park.

Opposite below: Seventeen-year-old Luther Cadogan driving a cart for Thomas and Evans Ltd, 1908. To meet the demands of a surging population a number of service industries had developed in the second half of the nineteenth century. Foremost among these new companies was the firm of Thomas and Evans Ltd. Its founder William Evans had come to the Rhondda from Pembrokeshire and in 1885 he started a grocery business in Hannah Street, Porth. Rapid and successful expansion soon followed and by the turn of the century he had formed a limited company with interests in butchery, baking and confectionery. Subsequently a jam factory and a mineral water concern, the Welsh Hill Works (later to develop into the Corona soft drinks company) were established and Thomas and Evans shops (aka Terry Stores) were opened throughout the Rhondda Valleys and elsewhere in Glamorgan.

Cymmer Colliery, opened by G. Insole & Son in 1877, seen here *c.*1920. The site is now occupied by
The Pioneer supermarket.

Opposite above: Weighers and other officials at Lewis Merthyr, 1920.

Opposite below: Unveiling of Trebanog mountain war memorial, Porth, 1919.

Porth and District Orchestral Society, 1927.

Bronwydd Park swimming pool, 1936. In 1922 William Evans, founder of Thomas and Evans Ltd, had given twenty acres of land to Rhondda District Council and this was subsequently developed as Bronwydd Park.

Opposite: Porth and District Chamber of Trade go for the "hard sell" during Porth's Empire Shopping Week, 15–21 March 1931.

This Booklet is full of Facts.

WISE FACTS! GOOD FACTS! SOUND FACTS!

IT'S A COMMON SENSE FACT—
That PORTH is the Best Shopping Centre.

IT'S A GEOGRAPHICAL FACT—
That " ALL Roads lead to PORTH."

IT'S A SCIENTIFIC FACT—
That a Straight Line is Bent.

IT'S A POSITIVE FACT—
That " Straight Folk " and " Bent Folk " when on Pleasure " Bent " go " Straight " to the Hub of Good Entertainment.

THE CENTRAL

PORTH'S IDEAL TALKIE CINEMA.

Pleasureable Programmes at Popular Prices always.

They come to Porth for Shopping Week,
The **Halt,** the **Lame**, the **Strong,** the **Meek** ;
Like the **CENTRAL**, **PORTH** is well renowned,
It serves you well, it's Goods are sound.

'S FACT.

Cymmer bridge, Porth, *c.*1900. This marked the boundary of the old parishes of Ystradyfodwg and Llantrisant.

Cymmer bridge, Porth, 1933.

Porth fire brigade's "christening" of a new fire engine, 1920s.

Porth Girls' School, 1936.

Rhondda Sea Cadets, Porth Division, 1949.

Opposite above: Land slip caused by severe flooding, Glynfach, Porth, 19-20 July 1939. The Terry Stores on the corner of Pleasant View is the building still standing to the right.

Opposite below: The high water mark at Cymmer bridge during the 1939 floods. The line was reached at 3 p.m. on 8 July.

Brittania Inn, Porth, 1950s.

Cymmer Colliery viewed from Porth bridge, 1950.

Porth Textiles Ltd, *c.*1950.

Remploy factory, Porth, 1953. In the 1945 Board of Trade development programme for the Rhondda provision was made for the employment of the disabled. This led to the building of two Remploy factories, one at Porth, and the other at Pentre.

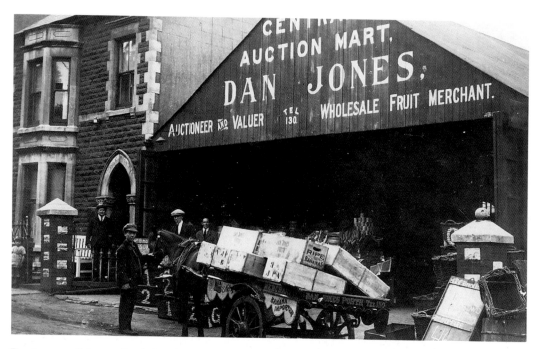

Dan Jones, well-known Porth fruit and vegetable wholesaler, 1920s. His son Cliff Jones was a Welsh rugby international.

Porth police station, 1989. Built in 1888 the building ceased to be used as a station in 1994.

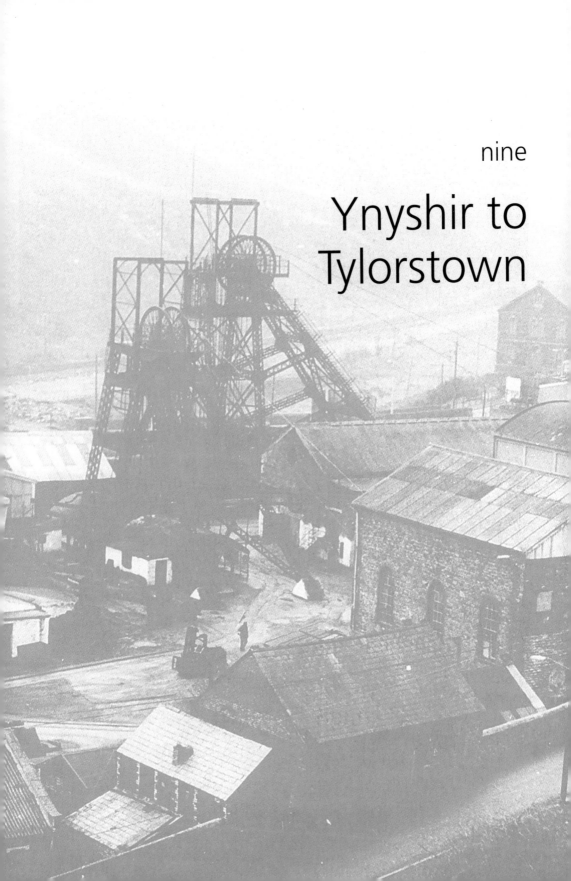

nine

Ynyshir to Tylorstown

Funeral procession for the victims of the explosion at No. 2 National Colliery, Wattstown which had claimed the lives of 119 workmen on 11 July 1905.

General view of Tylorstown showing Penrhys Road, Pleasant View and the police station, taken from above Stanleytown, c.1900.

Racing whippets at Gwernllwyn Terrace, 1910. From left to right, back row: Will Parfitt, George Thomas, R. Jones, –?–.Front row : Caleb Parfitt, Reubin Aplin, Morgan Parfitt, John Jones.

Tylorstown ambulance brigade, *c*.1912.

Tylorstown ambulance division, 1924, winners of the Peter Haig Thomas Challenge Shield and the Dr Glanville Morris Challenge Shield.

Holy Trinity AFC, Tylorstown, 1921-22 season.

Bowling green, Penrhys Park, Tylorstown, *c.*1930.

Committee of the No.7 lodge of the South Wales Miners' Federation (the "Fed"), Tylorstown, 1929. Back row: Llewelyn Jones, Morgan Thomas, William Wells, Thomas Maslin, Evan Morgan, Enoch Davies, Charles James. Third row: William Harries, David H. Evans, Trevor Hughes, Tom Hughes, Richard Parfitt, Rees Davies, David Williams, A.S. Rees, Thomas Davies. Second row: Robert ? , Evan Jones, William Parfitt, Richard Williams, Richard Perry, John E. Jones, Isaac Daniel, Thomas Gillgrass. Seated: William Evans, Daniel Rees, George Maslin.

East Road, Tylorstown, *c.*1910.

East Road, Tylorstown looking south-east, *c.*1910.

Above: Miners returning home along East Road, Tylorstown, *c*.1910.

Right: The Warren-Morgan family of Wattstown, *c*.1915. From left to right, back row: Mrs Ellen Warren-Morgan (mother), Nell, Lily. Front row: Nancy, Fred, Pincher the dog, Susan, Dolly, Violet. The photograph was taken to send to Private Joseph Warren-Morgan who was serving with the South Wales Borderers in the First World War. He was later elected Mayor of Rhondda Borough Council.

Last day at Wattstown Colliery, November 1968.

Opposite above: Wattstown old age pensioners' choir, *c.*1963, with conductor, Mr Matt Rowlands and accompanist, Miss Rosalie Wilson.

Opposite below: St Anne's church, Ynyshir, *c.*1970.

Wattstown Toreadors jazz band passing through Treorchy as part of the Pentre Carnival, 1973. Theresa Morgan was the drum major.

Soar Independent chapel, Pontygwaith, 1990. The new road will run along the old railway line.

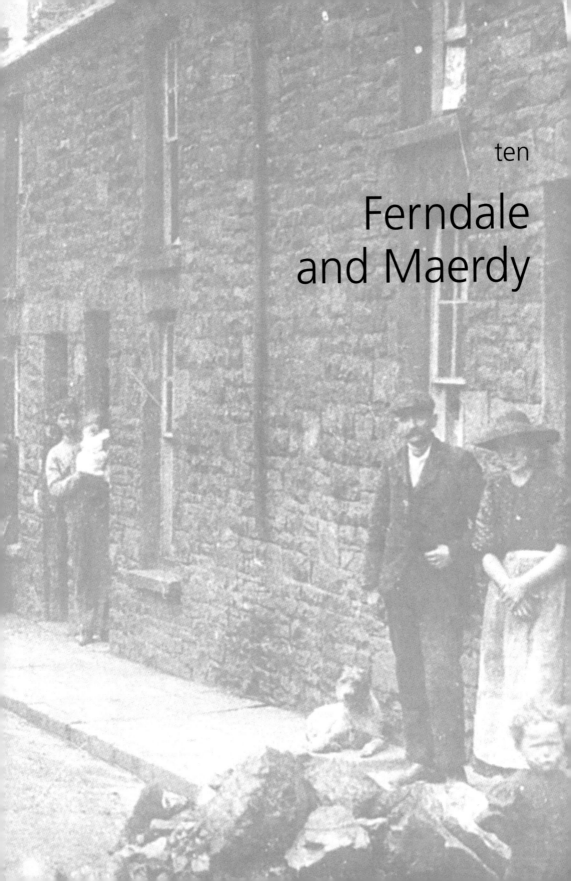

ten

Ferndale
and Maerdy

David Morgan's fleet of wagons for haulage and furniture removals, Wood Street, Ferndale, *c.*1900.

General view of Ferndale, *c.*1900.

No.1 and No.5 Ferndale collieries, *c.*1910. In 1867 the No.1 pit suffered the worst tragedy in the history of the Rhondda coalfield with 178 men killed after gas was ignited by the careless handling of a safety lamp. Two years years later a second major explosion ripped through the pit stealing a further 53 lives.

Charabanc outing from Ferndale, *c.*1910.

Mr Robert Thomas outside Blaenllechau Farm, *c.*1890. The farm is listed in the 1633 survey of the Manor of Penrhys.

View over Blaenllechau, *c.*1900.

Coal delivery at Long Row, Blaenllechau, *c.*1910.

Blaenllechau Radical Club rifle teams, 1912-13. From left to right back row: John Jones,
W.J. Jones (Secretary of Institute), James Protheroe (Vice-Chairman of Institute), Albert Gwillim
(Treasurer of Institute), Charles W. Pryce (Chairman of shooting league), Ernest Hughes (reserve).
Middle row: Richard Gilbert (Secretary of rifle team), Thomas Billings, John Evans (Captain),
George Bassett (Vice-Captain), David Cooper. Front row: John Harris (marker), Alfred Pulling.

Above: Maerdy Colliery, 1910. Four shafts were sunk here: Maerdy No.1 (1875), No.2 (1876), No.3 (1893) and No.4 (1914).

Right: Thirteen-year-old William David Jones of 2 Wood Street, Ferndale in his telegram boy uniform, *c*.1912.

Opposite: Maerdy tramcar, 1912. The first services operated by the Rhondda Tramways Co. Ltd opened in July 1908 between Trehafod and Partridge Road, in the Rhondda Fawr, and Pontygwaith in the Rhondda Fach. Such was the success of the new service that extensions to both lines were soon built. By April 1912 trams were able to run as far as Tynewydd and Maerdy.

The Strand, Ferndale, *c*.1910.

Gymnasium class of English Wesleyan church, 1912.

High Street, Ferndale, *c.*1920 with the Workmen's Hall clearly visible.

"Scrutting" for coal at Ferndale during the three month long lockout of the miners in 1921.

Volunteers who ran the Penuel chapel soup kitchen during the miners' strike, 1926. In reaction to employers' attempts to cut pay and alter working conditions a strike was called for 3 May and until 12 May it was supported by the TUC in a national general strike. The mineowners held out, however, and in December 1926 Welsh colliers returned to work in defeat having conceded the employers' demands.

Ferndale Labour Club Committee, 1933.

Left: Celebratory tea for the Coronation of George VI, Frederick Street, Ferndale, 1937.

Below: Ferndale Park tennis courts, *c.*1930, with from left to right: Mervyn Davies, Spencer Evans and Alfred Copley.

First coal risen at Bwllfa No.2, Mardy Colliery, 1952. As part of a development project a two and a half mile long tunnel had been driven through the mountain to link Mardy with the Bwllfa Colliery in the Cwmdare Valley.

Opening ceremony at Ferndale Library, 1966, with from left to right: Miss L.E. Gardner (Borough Librarian), W.D. Jones (Chairman, Libraries Committee), Alderman D. Murphy, the Mayor. The library was housed in the Workmen's Hall and Institute.

Banana Tip, Ferndale, 1978.

1991 view of the derelict Mardy Colliery site
showing the remains of the head gear and
winding wheel. Its closure the previous year
marked the end of deep mining in the
Rhondda valleys. In 1946 it was estimated that
over 1,000 million tons of coal remained to be
mined in the Rhondda. Where these reserves
have disappeared remains a mystery.

Acknowledgements

The authors would like to thank the following individuals and organisations for their help with the compilation of this book.

Rhondda Borough Libraries, in particular Susan Scott, Kay Warren-Morgan and Stephanie Thomas. Our research of the photographic archive at Treorchy library was made much more enjoyable and rewarding through their assistance and willing contribution of information. Many people have been responsible for building up the Treorchy collection, both local photographers and historians as well as members of the public. May we take this opportunity to thank them and also to invite the people of the Rhondda to carry on the good work by ensuring that, whenever possible, the images of their community's past are left in the safe and appreciative keeping of the library service. Here they will serve as a pool of memories and information for present and future generations. The Mayor of Rhondda Borough Council who has provided the book with an excellent introduction; George Vaughan (Treorchy); Dai Francis (Treherbert), Cllr., Mrs Iris Jenkins, the late Derek Clayton, the late Arthur Hazzard, Eileen Davies, Mr and Mrs Taylor, David Williams, T.B. Hughes, Mr W.R. Fox.